Fragments
of Survival

Poems by
Elizabeth Szewczyk

Fragments of Survival © 2017 Elizabeth Szewczyk. All rights reserved. Big Table Publishing Company retains the right to reprint. Permission to reprint must be obtained from the author, who owns the copyright.

ISBN: 978-1-945917-22-6

Printed in the United States of America

Front cover image, *Dreamscape: Moonlit,* courtesy of Alex Keto
Author photo is by Tom Szewczyk

Also by Elizabeth Szewczyk:

This Becoming

"Making other books jealous since 2004"

Big Table Publishing Company
Boston, MA
www.bigtablepublishing.com

For Allison, Tommy, Jessica, Dan,
and for my God daughter, Jillian.
And for Tom, always, always, always.

"A scar does not form on the dying. A scar means, I survived."
~ Chris Cleave

Table of Contents

Prologue
    What I Know
    The Changeling

Part One
The Beginning	13
Lost	14
Portrait of an Abuser as a Young Boy	15
Apple Picking	16
Past the Imaginary Line	17
Exile	18
Winter	19
The Separation	20
Shame	21
Rules of the Kingdom	22
Willow	23
Nourishing the Hating Seed	24
What I Keep	25
Sold	26
Returning Home to Innocence	27
Ravaged	28
Haunted	29
Released	30
Unforgotten	31
Journal	32
What Might Have Been	33

Part Two
Masked	37
Ping-Pong	38
Curriculum	39
Visitation	40
Knitting	41

Faces in the Window	42
Transmutation	43
Shattered	44
Autumn Light Setting Fire	45
When I Tell You the Secret, Darling	46
The Abyss	47
In Praise of Silence	48
Black Curtain	49
Utterance of Emergence During Daytime	50
Redemption	51
Harbor Side	52
Metamorphosis	53
Morning	54
The Promise	55
Reflections in Moonlight	56
Reporting	58
Peace	59
Unwavering	60
Salvation	61

What I Know

How hard she must have pushed me through,
my eyes biting the light, forcing my lids
to close like doors of a house bullied by the North wind.
I think now, *How did I bear this?*
Marked and wet, the warmth was gone,
that whooshing lullaby gone,
everything safe, stripped and cut.
They printed and tagged me, pinched
scarlet blood from my heel, announced

my sex to the world. Then bundled
in soft cloth, they laid me on her breast,
her palm soothing the fontanelle of my head,
her air whisking into my nose and mouth,
her breath calling the name gifted to me.
What I know is her voice was familiar,
I knew her well.

Changeling

She's the child you watched
kneeling on the wooden pew
each Sunday, her fists balled
and white, peeking above her gloves,
praying to the crucified Christ.

She's the child you wished to be,
dressed in patent leather shoes
and lace socks, beaded pocketbooks
and pink crinoline.
In your torn tights and scuffed

Buster Browns, you lowered
your face, counted the marble
tiles between rows, longed
to wear her shoes.
She sat smoothing her dress,

knowing night would fall
and another day rise, until
loneliness caught like a tornado,
blew dank air into her face
while you played in dirt

with friends who dressed their dolls
in cotton rags and paper, sat
holding hands, laughing,
touching shoulders, knees,
while she went home, clean, alone.

Part One

"Today my forest is dark. The trees are sad and
all the butterflies have broken wings."
~ Raine Cooper

The Beginning

Fifty years later, I think
of the year when childhood faded
like the face of an old photo,
dressed itself in shadows,
snuffed faces, tiny tears
left between the paper of development
until the images evaporated into dust,
cracks from another era.
For a short time, within the meadow
of seeded grass and wild roses, I was a child,
innocent and pure, trusting all who called me
to them, ready to embrace that rare love
of abstinence and purity without fear
or happenstance. For a short time,
the moon was simply a stone to gaze upon
and stars were lights without wishes.
The world was small and innocent and I
crossed the imaginary line without a care.
Gladiolas danced in daylight like they'd
never wilt in secret, bees buzzed in
the honeycombs, butterflies sprang
from cocoons. And there I was,
a young child, waiting for life to open.

Lost

In the forest, giant oaks surround you,
wrap weather-laden arms around you,
green spruce piercing branches and needles
between layers of delicate skin.
Miles of velvet blankets fill their floor,
false havens of rest, enticing
unsuspecting souls to linger longer.
They pull you in, these counterfeit
coverings of safety.
Beware.
They masquerade, become dark knights
and you wander naively through as
dusk reveals Master Moon.
His light folds you with bewildered senses,
steals your hope.
Don't think Mother will hear you,
keep you safe.
On this path, she isn't here.

Portrait of an Abuser as a Young Boy

He is six years old, playing with three-
inch metal trucks, crashing them across
the asphalt sidewalk in front
of his home, until they bottom-up
in summer grass, cracking plastic
windows that hold tin figures inside.
He opens the truck's doors, checks
to see that the half-inch men kiss
the steering wheel before he abandons
the trucks to the street. A car screeches
to a halt. It dents the toy's edges,
crushes a wheel or maybe the whole front,
while he applauds.

His mother runs outside and wagging
a finger, screams *There won't be new trucks
for a looong time*, calls him *reckless*, does he
think their family is made of money?
Silent, he gathers the ruined trucks like eggs,
folds them deep into his shirt, buries them
in the corner side of the house, by the gladiolas,
then plants the Hating Seed, waters with tears.

Apple Picking

Mother puts a quarter
in my hand and I walk with friends
to the apple farm.
Cortland is my favorite, the crunchy skin,
sweet juice dripping onto my tongue.
Holding the pulp inside my cheek
I savor the sour after-bite.
On the way home we cross the street,
loose baby teeth whittling
apples into core and seed.

A man, dressed in plaid flannel shirt and blue jeans
is waving, sitting on the concrete steps of the house
around the corner, flicking ashes from
his cigarette onto daisies growing by his feet.
I wonder why he'd dirty such pretty flowers.

Next fall my friends will return to the apple grove
while I wait ahead of the corner, tell them
I don't eat apples anymore.

Past the Imaginary Line

That October, as leaves began their downward
spiral, musty piles on piles, summer evaporating
into autumn's darkness, I roamed.
Past wilted gladiolas,
past picked-over corn stalks,
past the Imaginary Line my mother
warned me not to cross, to where
grass was obsolete and ants devoured
beetle carcass on cement steps.

Steel slammed—Whack!
(the wind caught the door).
No candy? No gum? No "Little Lulu"?
Scuffed patent leathers thrashed,
never worn again.

Goodbye gladiolas
(Mother wrenched the bulbs from her garden).
Blood-soaked lace socks and buckled shoes
held tightly to her breast, while ants devoured
beetle carcass on cement steps.

Exile

From the falling mounds
of apples, rotted pumpkins,
ice-bitten gladiolas, throw
in a cornstalk, bare, unyielding corn.

Now crush them, release
these organics, each orphaned,
bruised, dying after
the fertile harvest.

I never knew cornstalks cried,
never cast away apples and
pumpkins while worms feasted
their seeds. What remains?

It came so quietly, no one
heard the taps a child makes
upon the earth when the season
of childhood is dying.

Winter

My snowsuit lay unworn, hat and mittens
stuffed inside the pockets, black rubber
boots, shiny as new ornaments on Christmas
trees, the words, "Don't touch" invisible
and unspoken.

I stayed inside, locked myself in a room
where teddy bears whispered secrets
and cherished dolls closed their eyes
in tiny cribs and carry-ons, afraid to see
the mysteries mid-day placed between
the parallel houses.

My mother was preparing for a new baby,
decorating bassinets and folding receiving
blankets. My father was busy working to give
his young family all he'd promised. At night
I'd sit by my bedroom window, watch my neighbor
dry his dinner dishes, hands gliding around the edges,

feel the calloused fingers on my legs as he dried
me that October, when I had been his.

Shame

The socks were hung
three seasons of the year,
in sun that made them glitter
like fluorescent kites, wind
drinking their wetness, flapping
in pale blue sky.

At first, the socks were stained
cotton candy pink, spun in lines
where a tissue wiped the wounds
cut days before.

Later the pink turned raspberry,
and Mother bleached them,
tried to hide the desperation.
She would soak each cotton sock
until they tinted water like the Red Sea,
then opened the drain, released
almost everything.

The Separation

In early spring, Father builds the wooden
fence, the house behind it barely visible.
He digs through Mother's garden, scoops
the imaginary gate full of pansies, rose bushes.

All weekend he measures, saws and nails,
buzzing through our tiny neighborhood,
arousing curiosities. Ours is the first fence.
The neighbors gather, can't imagine why.
They don't have a pool.

I watch from my bedroom window,
the metal door so familiar, its screen
carved with holes the size of a child's finger,
hear the pitch of the band saw sizzle, watch

the deep crevices where my mother's garden
grew, fill with wood, wonder how some boards
will protect.

Rules of the Kingdom

In summer we built a castle in the woods,
on thick branches where maples
and oaks stood guard, and embedded
stones became gates.

We pulled a worn sheet, frayed edges,
faded from too many washings, over
the branches, stopping midway, where
leaves became a hidden screen,

and the dirt below camouflaged
our suntan legs.
Enter in the back and be quiet.
This is where you hide from the enemy.

Then I closed the castle doors with
wooden clothespins, patted my friend's backs,
pretended I was their queen, keeping
my treasured Subjects safe.

Willow

At my grandfather's lake, the willow trees
swing their leaves, sweep the graceless ground
where reeds grow in murky water and I dream
of floating away, dream of cool swells cleansing
everything that has been drenched with dirt.

The willows hide my face from the sky.
I could close my eyes and never open them,
slide my feet beneath the bank, hear the willows
whisper goodbye.
Render myself gone.

Nourishing the Hating Seed

With age, his life grew more pathetic:
At twelve, he sits in a middle school classroom,
acne circling his face, strings of hair on his chin
and lips. His teacher calls his name and the room
is silent, an air of waiting.
That morning his mother mumbled something
about how he had better grow up, that she
was sure *he'd be a Nothing*.

After school, he owns the house
until suppertime.
A snack, comic books, a nap.
At dusk he drags his feet to the garden,
where the Hating Seed is planted. Watering
until drenched, he pulls the leaves from its branches.
It flourishes, grows thicker each day.

What I Keep

"In the present is the past."
  ~ Albert Einstein

Books about princesses and princes. Dolls in pinafores and lace, socks and shoes white as shaved ice. Friendly faces, toothy smiles, chestnut braided hair with red gingham bows. Sunshine through autumn leaves, evergreen trees holding Christmas lights. My baby brother bundled in blue, Mother dressed in tan wool knits and two-strand alabaster pearls. My father, black suit and red striped tie, kneeling for hugs, brass-locked leather briefcase, bags of frosted gumdrops under his arms. My seventh birthday, chocolate cake and yellow candles, fingers gliding through icing. Flowered underwear tied with satin ribbons, lavender bubble bath, a jump rope with purple handles, white and blue checked sneakers.

I keep myself clean, showers steaming each pore,
scouring away his fingers, breath, words.

Sold

One day, there it was, written
as news headlines. I was eight,
aware that the sign sealed his
leaving, "Sold" plunged into
the middle of dry weedy grass.
The fingerprints had disappeared,
curtains removed, yard tools non-existent.
Everything was vacant, wilted, neglected.
He had disappeared into the night.
I stored the story in a locked safe, thinking
my childhood would return, pure as new
snow, a fence marking the Invisible Line.
Really, I knew it would remain caught
in the memories like plastic suffocates
the sea turtle, inescapable,
the Hating Seed left behind, imperceptible.

Returning Home to Innocence

We traveled back the summer
I was twelve, to visit the place where
we had lived that first winter, snow
drifts covering front doors, billowing

tree tips and telephone wires.
How strange it looked. Dark and bold,
foliage shadowing roofs, hiding secrets
behind leaves, and air so still, so warm,

neighbors stripped their clothes without
any notion of having sex.
How could this be the place? Once we
stood tightly, just the three of us,

calm, content, my mother's waist
slim and cinched, auburn hair scooping
her shoulders, ruby lips framing white teeth.
My father, a head taller, uniformed green,

metal wings above his left breast pocket,
a pilot's cap clutched between his elbow
and hip, a glint in his eyes, waiting for
the camera to snap his young family.

And I, bundled so securely, only the pink
cheeks of my face spilled out of my bunting.
Twelve years later, I filtered this image onto
the flat black pavement, heat steaming its cracks

while full-bloomed roses wilted between
faded fence slats.

Ravaged
~ For Bill

He asks me how I know these children
are no longer children, although they look
like children, age like children,
speak like children.
I tell him it's their eyes, hollow rings,
dark circles of implausible sadness,
the discovery that something inside
has changed, become undone.

I tell him there are invisible mirrors
around their perimeter, broken, like cracks
on the ice pond in winter. They glimpse
each other's reflections, know the fear
of drowning,
weep when one has fallen through.

Haunted

There are days the house calls.
The Present vanishes.
I am six, standing among purple pansies
in my mother's garden, hear him
whisper my name from his door.
The imaginary line separates us,
warns me not to listen.
Corn husks curl and cry.

Now, only weeds remain,
the result of abandon, a walkway
of wilted leaves and garbage.
I see a door with swirls, red and black,
a screen torn and battered.
A child's smeared handprint, begging to escape.

Released

Even now,
when leaves begin to free
themselves, I am mesmerized
by the colors they implode—
red, orange, yellow, purple—
when they are near their end.

These veiny tissues entrance,
pull me into their chlorophyll wake,
as the air sweeps their skeletons
beside the trunk where they
were born.

They brown and crisp, crumble,
wait to become dust. It is time
to rake them into earthly caskets,
finish the death watch of what was once beautiful.

Unforgotten

The memories water my body
like my mother watered gladiolas,
drenched them from the tips of
their silken heads to the roots of
their feet until they drooped, exhausted,
their petals withered.

His face is a mystery now,
a thin veil of time hiding the hue
of his hair. Brown? Black?
It doesn't matter. In my dreams
he slinks to my side, his mouth
a garden hose spraying in my ear—
Good girl. Now you can have the candy.

Journal

Unfolding each dog-eared page,
I open words written by memories,
beige colored, and transform them
by igniting embers, fires in a haunted past,
that would reel through my body,
until each memory tore the heart,
until each penned word left a feeling of cause
to end the emptiness that rang and blanketed
everything dead inside.
And this madness fed the soul until visible
to others, I arose in fury.

What Might Have Been

What if he had first appeared, tall and soft-spoken,
sampling summer fruit at the neighborhood stand?
Would he have set the ripe fruit in a woven basket,
noticed unstained sneakers on the tiny feet?
Gold metallic barrettes Mother carefully clipped
onto braided hair that morning? The way her mouth
widened, deciding peaches over plums?
What if he looked without dressing this child, saw
a six-year old who simply liked to smile?
What if our paths crossed that day and life
never wove between our bodies again?

Part Two

"I have learned now that while those who speak about one's miseries usually hurt, those who keep silence hurt more."
~ C.S. Lewis

Masked

When I put the mask on,
kept my face inside,
it was easier *to be*,
knowing it would shield
my abused identity.
Behind the mask,
my eyes blackened, like
charcoal left in its bag
too long, unable to be lit,
sparked. My nostrils closed
tight, extinguished the sweet
smells of spring rain and
summer flowers.
A slit of space exposed
my mouth, sipped bits
of air, molecular leftovers.
What to do now? I shuffled
past people without unveiling,
sure they wouldn't notice what lay
behind the mask, sure they wouldn't
wonder why it never unhinged,
my handiwork a masterpiece of deception.

Ping Pong

No one feels the fear, hears
voices paddle ping pong
through the mind, a back
and forth motion of disconcerted
tension. Each a mystifying vat
of energy, untiring, unquenched,
unselected. Whispers wallowing
in my head, chattering conversations,
vying to be the one not ignored,
the one given attention.

And I, unable to answer *No*,
surrender to that voice.

Curriculum

A lifetime has passed since I met him.
Today is the first day of school and I
am their teacher. The coat closets gleam
from Clorox. GI Joe and Barbie book bags
hang on polished gold hooks, as my second grade
students call out their names, pink gummy windows
where teeth have vacated mouths,
fingers wrinkled from too much bath water last night,
honeysuckle and lavender aromas coveting their heads.

They are waiting to know.
What will I teach them?

Share your crayons, offer half
a snack to classmates who forget
theirs, don't count sips at the water
faucet, be patient in the lunch line.

And most important, learn to say *No*
when danger approaches, that uncomfortable touch
pleading for their most intimate parts.
Run, I tell them. *Run.*

Visitation

No one knew how to approach.
Bringing food and flowers, expensive
bottles of perfume, they visit with their
own thoughts while eating, smelling, spraying,
saying nothing about those months.
We don't want to upset her.
They leave quickly and quietly.

Staring out the windows surrounding
the cage, I focus on the snow melting
into the earth. Spring will be calling
the birds back. The sun will heat my face.
Soon it will be time for the fifteen-minute
walk in the gated, manicured yard.

Knitting

The woman, speechless and intent,
has sat in the chair for five days,
knitting the same row of yarn,
thumbs and fingers wrapping the air,

loops running over and up, drop
one stitch, pick another.
They call her The Factory Worker,
so determined to finish this last row

before the whistle hollers and the supervisor
folds her hands into her lap, stuffs
invisible yarn and needles into a bag,
tells her she has earned her pay today.

Faces in the Window

It's true, they all look the same.
Cheeks doughy like pie pastry,
lips fallen caverns.
Their hair twirls between fingers,
strings like twine falling into bloodshot eyes.

Do I look like them?
I can't tell. Mirrors are forbidden,
guard against sharp edges used
to slice scarred skin.
A reflection in the window calls
my name. No answer.

Blood drips from gnawing lips.
Is it too late to breathe fresh air?

Transmutation

The woman in the hospital corner
spreads her legs like she is giving birth
to a ghost, tilts her head until her mouth
gapes and silently screams into the air
while we stare, our eyes fixated above
her head, waiting to glimpse the sibilant
spirit infecting every life form within.

This is not a cleansing.
This is not a redemption.
This is body and spirit possessed,
a woman captured,
her past purged into present.

Shattered

After years of silence, my mind
buried itself like a coffin, closed
the cover and latched the past.
The child inside the woman glued
her mouth long ago, her body a cube
of glass, afraid it would be tapped
and shattered.
Such a shame, the doctors agreed.
So bright and talented, wondering how
to make her whole after all those years.
The woman listened, pondered their words,
watched the steel doors lock, then vomited
her childhood on the cold, tiled floor.

Autumn Light Setting Fire

What do we do when seasons capture us,
imprison the spirit in our bodies? Outside
my kitchen window squirrels scamper,
fill their nests before the dark quilt of winter
covers the earth.

I want their strength,
want to build my nest brighter,
basket weave the edges so it
glows in moonlight.

I want a nest of light,
fire red leaves blazing,
sparking amber in my eyes,
filling my mind with
Yes, good light, yes.

When I Tell You the Secret, Darling,

assure me this isn't the summit,
that the course will be longer, we'll carry
our swollen feet through the rough terrain,
cross the crest of this mountain.

If you thirst with questions, I will hold
the flask to your lips, nourish your throat,
offer answers one at a time until
you are satisfied and full.

Will your soul explode with grief?
Lock your fingers around mine,
rub them like flint until they spark,
ignite what we have pieced together.

The Abyss
~ *For Tom*

Watching your face dissolve
into exhaustion is the hardest part.
I want to open your eyes, half-mast
and wet with worry, tell you this will pass.

Take you in my arms, hold you
when this isn't sifting every
muscle and nerve into sand high as
the dunes that dwell by the ocean.

If I could, I would destroy
these demons, stretch their cells
beyond the darkness, bury them in
dirt where we'd never walk.

Don't say *We're blessed*, that *this is
just the way it's meant to be.*
The ground is growing soft with spring.
Shouldn't winter be over?

In Praise of Silence

Tonight no music plays, my mind is all alone.
Each synapse in my brain lies idle and content.
The walls inside are dark and still. Mozart is not home.

Who knows the brain from sight? The tone
of each word spoken? The heart accepts
tonight no music plays, my mind will be alone.

No symphonies grasp chords unknown
like a gasping voice anonymously swept
within cerebral walls, when Mozart is not home.

Conductor waves words within every bone,
shadows of darkness upon me crept
at night, but music doesn't play, my mind is all alone.

What joy to wake at day without the moan
of violins inside my depths,
and laugh at walls, dark and still, since Mozart is not home.

And banish this symphony few have known,
the years pass by and I've kept track
of nights no music plays, peaceful and alone,

when walls inside are dark and stilled,
and Mozart is not home.

Black Curtain

Beyond this invisible black curtain
suspended like a blanket covering the head,
torso, toes, is the sparrow of sunlight,
perched and ready to enter, bring its singing
bright light to the nest where life waits.

Music, laughter, the composition of wholeness
remains outside this blanket, longs to relieve
the dark forcing the deaf, mute, blind.
Can there be a more tender waiting?

One by one the people will celebrate,
assume she is well. Her hair, eyes, lips will shine
with color, fool the uninformed.
They will think there is little amiss.
Perhaps she is tired. Perhaps she is bored.

But the curtain stays and the blanket wraps
tighter, darker. There will be little relief
from seamless midnight. Fly then, sparrows
and you who are unaware. Leave her to dwell
within the shadows. Leave her.

Utterance of Emergence During Daytime
~ The Egyptian Book of the Dead

How long does a damaged life
murmur before it surrenders?
For years they weighed this heart,
its sounds a whisper, pronounced

me dead and inscribed my name
on papyrus. Their guilt sorrowed me
into the underworld, cast me
into the Hall of Ma'at, heavy

and condemned. When all appeared
lost, you rescued me from darkness,
reclaimed the heart, carried me
to the Field of Reeds.

Redemption
~ For Tommy

I could not comfort him the morning
he showed himself, my first born son,
his eyes shut from the fear
of long cuts the doctor made,

twisting and pulling, releasing him
from me. I was present but absent,
my mind a nothingness of thought, the gas
flowing through my paralyzed body,

bound in a dream- less dream.
He didn't know me then, cleaned
and covered by stranger's hands,
blood dripping from the severed stem

that held us together. He was alone,
and there I lay, my womb exposed
to all of them, the intimate cavern
we shared for months. Hours later,

they gave him to me, his soft clean
skin nuzzled at my cheeks, warm air
of his breath filling my lungs,
the sight of him holy and pure.

I was like Eve, my sins forgiven
for this great love.

Harbor Side

The walls are drying, blue paint covering
gold you never liked, couldn't get used to,
although for me, the color was regal.

Nailing white wainscoting halfway up,
because the colors soothe together, it
reminds me of the harbor side, where

white sand meets blue water, and swimmers
mush both on their bodies.
You can feel the grains of sand clutter

in toes and hair, relentless bits while
stepping into water, bodies cleaning
their palates to be painted again.

Water drips into sand, brushes every
corner and crevice of skin, renewing
the body with foaming

waves until the sun melts
them together, clots them into one.
We are like sand and water, mushing

together in our lives. I'll be sand,
while you cover me in blue.

Metamorphosis

In summer, a caterpillar crawled
in the grass, or maybe on the sidewalk,
unscathed by birds or human feet.
Pure luck.
Wrapping itself in a cocoon,
the caterpillar waits, unsure of its fate,
considering at times the effort to live,
remembers only life bound in this
mummy-like covering.

As the metamorphosis takes hold,
the cocoon unwraps,
sinewy strings that held it prisoner.
Peering down, the caterpillar notices
wings, and color, and antennae
sprouted to feel the world in a different way.
An unexpected change has come, everything
unique to its second life.
It is like Lazarus, come forth from
the cave for a second chance.

Morning
~ For J

Be calm, child.
This dark vault of sorrow
won't see the morning.
Look toward the moon,
shooting stars, ask them
to grant wishes.
Dawn will erode
each locked door of anguish.
Trust what I say.
Then wait for the pouring rain.
It will pelt the dust, cleanse.

The Promise
~ For Dan

Before I realize the magnitude of sorrow,
our youngest son flails into my arms,
fingers indenting my shoulders like
a life jacket unclaimed, his lifeboat
sinking a foot away.

He's taken the call, our friend is gone,
couldn't bear his life's pain. Once again,
sorrow bursts into my son's young life,
saturating his fears. I bundle him in my arms
as I did when he was born, salt water

and soft howling rising from his spirit,
whisper, *shhhh, shhhh,* his black hair
splintering my eyes, chest heaving
with timeless breath.

Later, he rubs the wet, cradles my face
with soaked fingers, a reverberation
of gasping sounds echoing in his throat.
"I won't," I whisper in his left ear,

my mind mapped with his thoughts,
so afraid to meet his eyes to mine.
"I promise." A covenant is made.
"I promise. I won't."

Reflections in Moonlight
~ For Jillian

On that winter's night,
light glistened on fresh snow
and we twirled, black velvet, red
ribbons, our shadows mirrored in moonlight,
no voice between us, just silence
surrounding movement, dancing.

Faster and faster until the dance
dizzied our heads and the night
stirred dark memories, your silent
tears casting crevices in snow.
I held your hand in moonlight,
delicate fingernails painted red,

the air of our silence
broken when you opened red
cuts from chaffed lips, bleeding in snow.
Our minds raced as the dancing
frenzied, memories of nightmares,
innocence taken by others in moonlight.

I had never been comforted in moonlight,
never wrapped my arms silently
around a child whose nightmares
were the same as mine, ready
to tell my story as we danced,
watching your tears turn to crystals in snow,

stream down your cheeks, snowing
like diamonds in moonlight,
while our dancing
feet grew weary and worn. This night couldn't silence
our grief, bring our souls redemption
from the torment, but on this night

we ceased gazing into haunted mirrors, snowflakes
cleansing the mind's past, silently.
Noticing the glow of lovely moonlight
we watched your ragged red
lips heal from the night's
beams of warm light as we ended the dance.

There was moonlight and us, dressed in red and black,
"Silent Night" playing softly, snowflakes dancing.

Reporting
~ For Jessica

Today you meet me flushed and tear-filled,
grieving gulps of sorrow
like your love has died, like the smooth
grain of your flesh will dissolve.
Rushing toward my shoulders, every breath
an explosion of hiccups, you tell me how
it hurt to make the call, The Call to save them.

I see your heart exposed, the open wound
of muscle behind your shirt. You knew
what to say, how to distance
yourself from the scene. That perfect
combination of love and justice.

And still, today, the problem punishes,
reduces you to my baby, the child
who's fearful of the dark alone.
I rub your back, fingers fanned
to reassure your breath,

to reassure what you did
was right. *You were the brave one,*
my child,
and all I really want to do
is cradle your head and croon lullabies.

Peace

On Sundays we go to that same church
that preaches forgiveness, the church
I went to as a child, when the howling happened.
Looking around, there are familiar faces,
older and wrinkled, familiar bodies
holding canes and walkers, their bones
riddled with holes from age.

I am older too. More than fifty years past that year.
My knees drop to the cushion and gazing
to the cross, I know it is time to let him go.
He's an old man by now, if he lives. A lifetime
filled with anger and fear hold his heart,
a loveless life.

In the stained glass, rays of sun
stream, light the small corners
that hide the dark, fall away
from crowded shadows.
I know he remembers.
Peace, I say to his ghost.

Unwavering
~ For Allison

Whenever the light falters and
blackness invades my weary self,
you wrap me in kindness, assure every
part of my torn self that I am worthy.
Who taught you to do this? Who graced
you with unconditional love? Like the oceans
you visit, we watch the waters capture our
silence, the magnitude of life breathe through
its crest, yet your spirit never wavers from the tide,
never drifts away, my child.

Salvation

The fluids inside my body,
raged from the firestorm,
raveled through crevices,
seared my bones, muscles,
my sex. There was no vapor
of air. Even my soul smoked
from fire.

Past the years, smeared with
soil and ash, I woke
to one redeeming morning,
heard the drone of bees drunk
from thick nectar,
noticed leaves glistening green.
Ruby ripe strawberries
made my tongue cry.
The wounds were healing,
the scars fading more each day.

I felt my face, unclamped the mask,
became who I was meant to be.

Acknowledgements

No one writes a book by themselves. Books are the result of hundreds (if not thousands) of hours, relying on many people from start to publication. *Fragments of Survival* is the completion of eight years of poetry, testing time and intimacy these poems reveal. I want to thank first, my daughter, Allison McKeen, whose writing I've admired since she held a pen, for giving me the "final push" to submit this manuscript. To Edwina Trentham and Steve Straight, who workshopped many poems in their earliest forms. To Gay Paluch, Vivianne Grabinski and Paige Steinert, members of my earlier writing group. To Tracy Capello, for her support and honesty with my most recent poems. To Elaine Bristol, who listens with constant patience. To my daughter, Jessica Russell, a true "hero", whose professional work protects these children. To Jillian, whose bravery let me tell her story too. My sons, Tommy and Dan, who listened to this painful telling, and who have grown into men who would make any mother proud. To my beloved Tom, for hearing these poems over and over in rewrite; I know it broke your heart, but you saved me by encouraging me to write this. Thank you to John, Rebecca, and Chloe, for your gracious time and reviews; I am humbled. To my favorite Editor, the brilliant Robin Stratton, who patiently waited for me to have the courage to send this out, and who worked with me every step of the way, giving me a platform to speak my truth. Finally, to all of the sexually abused children who think no one is listening. We are.

www.ingramcontent.com/pod-product-compliance
Lightning Source LLC
LaVergne TN
LVHW041309080426
835510LV00009B/930